Color My Blessings

An Abstract Coloring Book

By

Christi Wells

Color My Blessings: An Abstract Coloring Book

Cover and interior design by Christi Wells | fromthesprings.com

ISBN-13: 978-1534809116

ISBN-10: 1534809112

To those who have discovered

the meditative joy of adult coloring books

and wish to try a more challenging approach

that will enhance their creative skills, I invite you to

Color My Blessings.

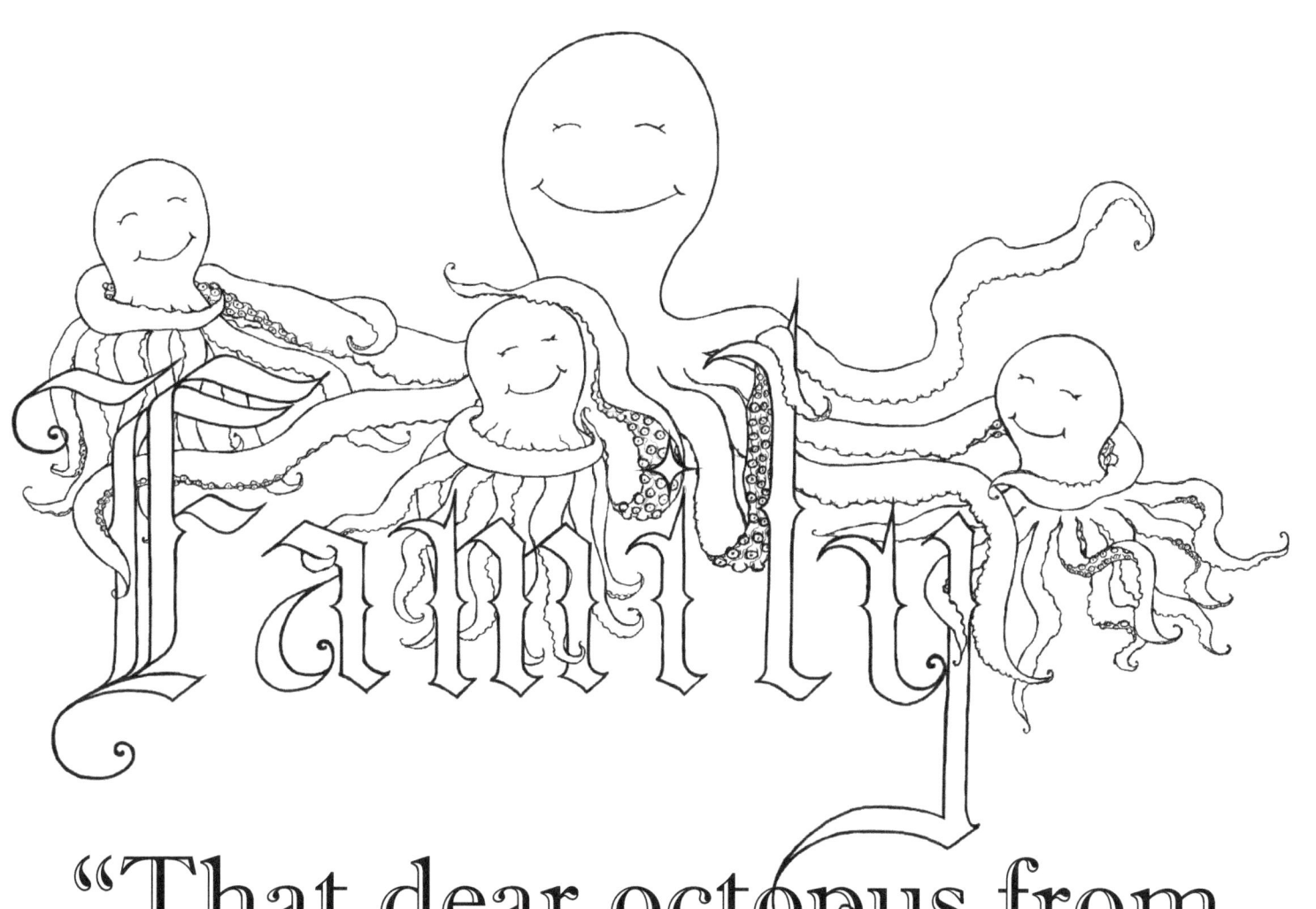

"That dear octopus from whose tentacles we never quite escape, nor in our inmost hearts ever quite wish to."
-Dodie Smith

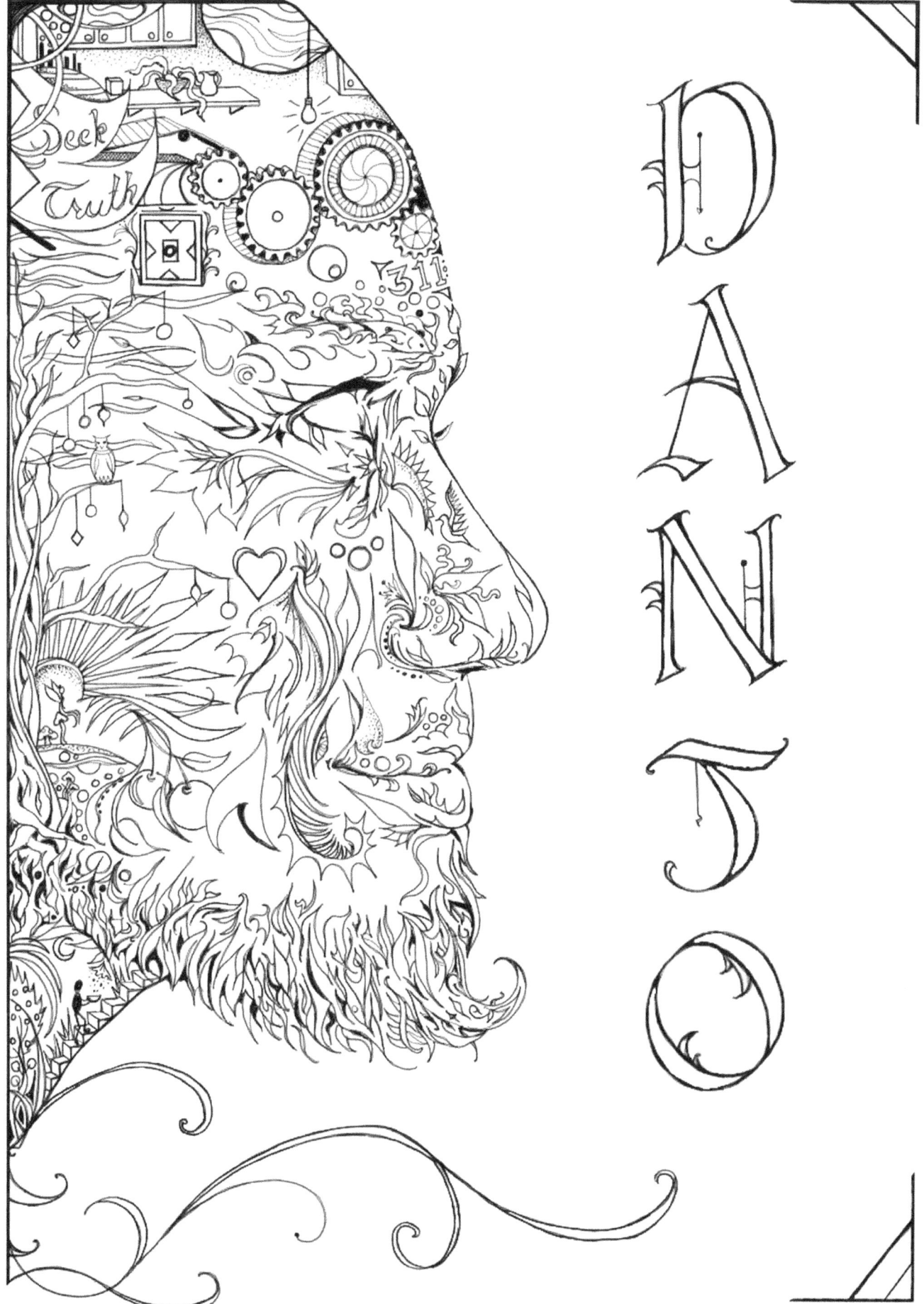

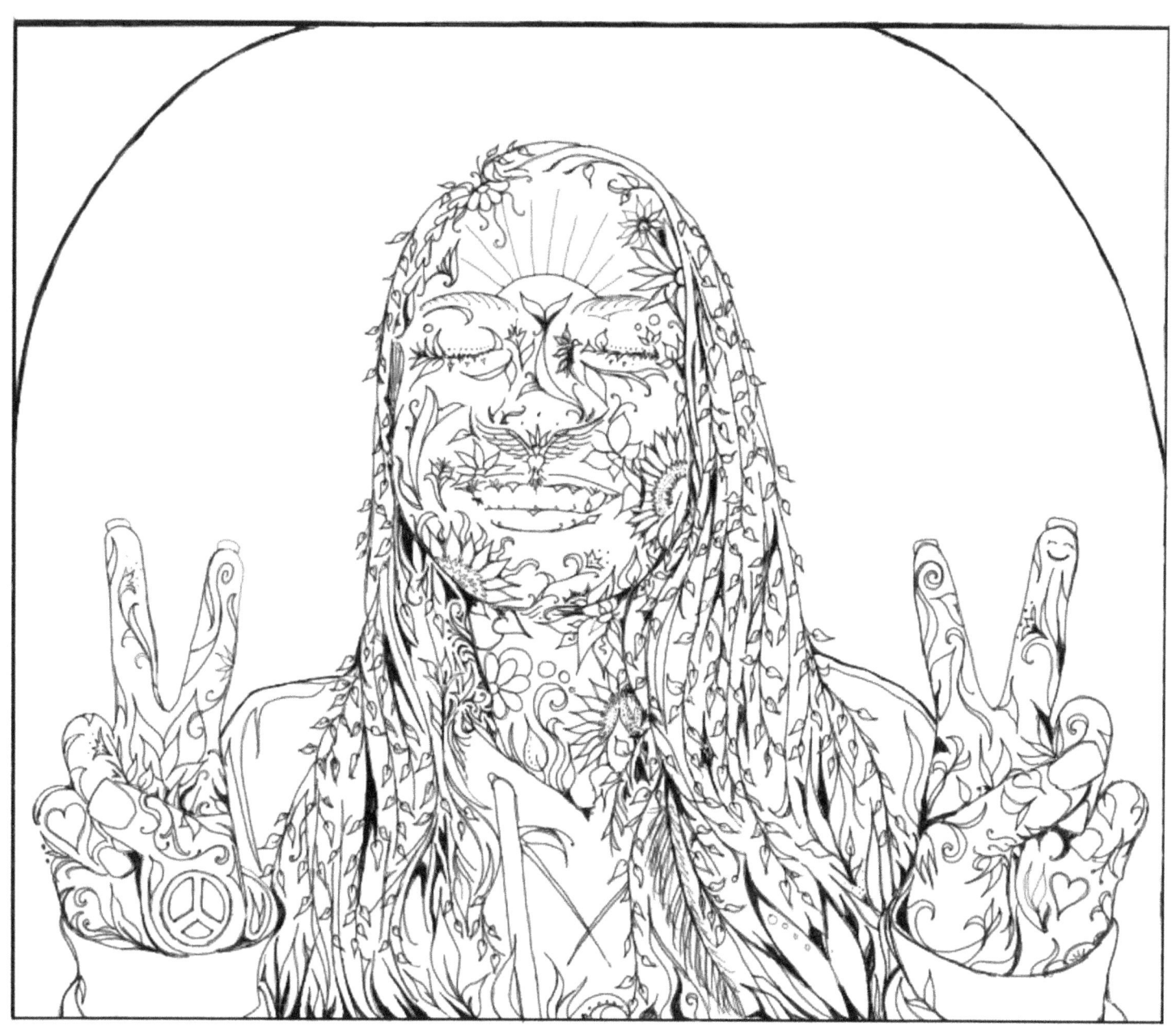

Maya

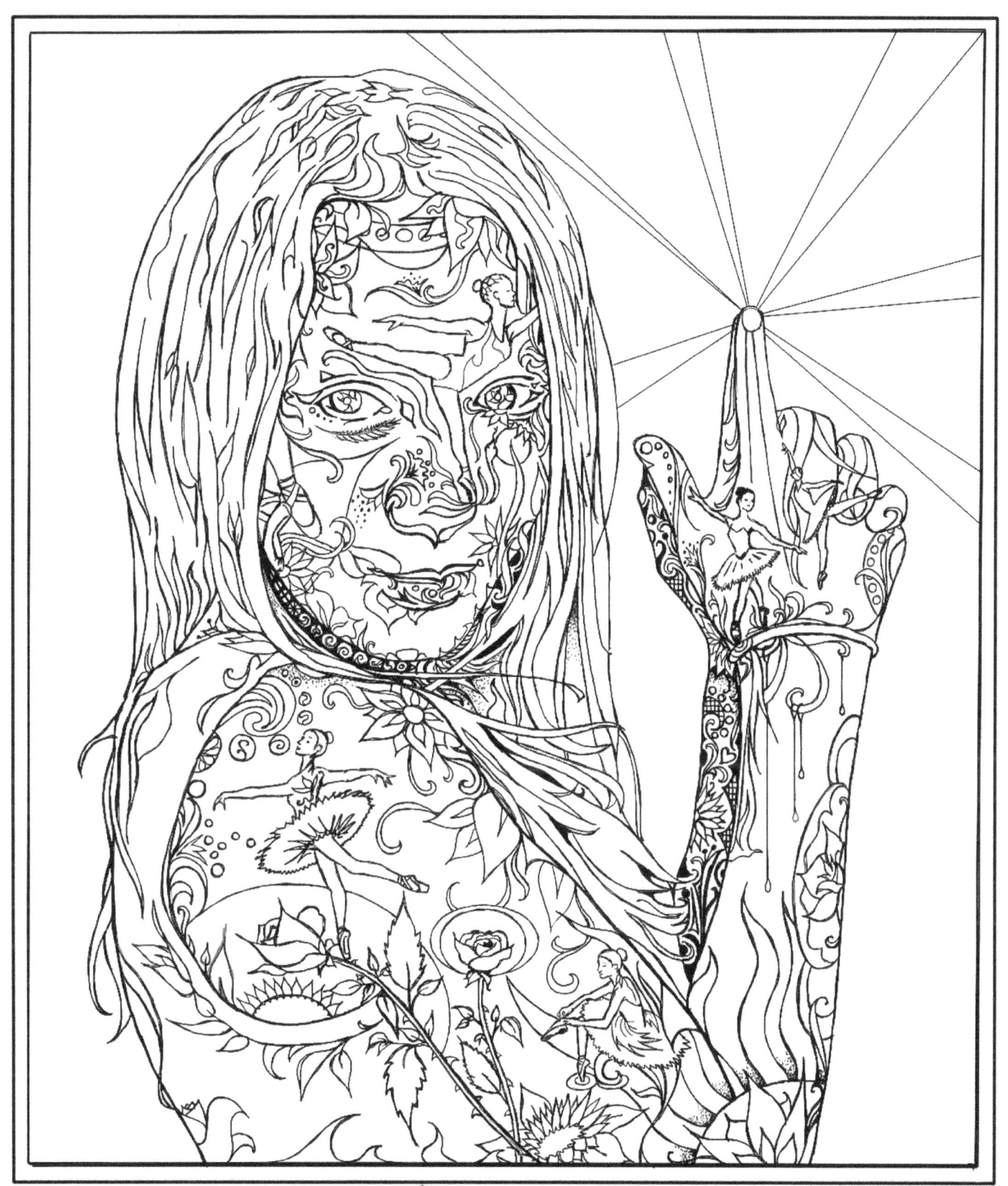

Ziona

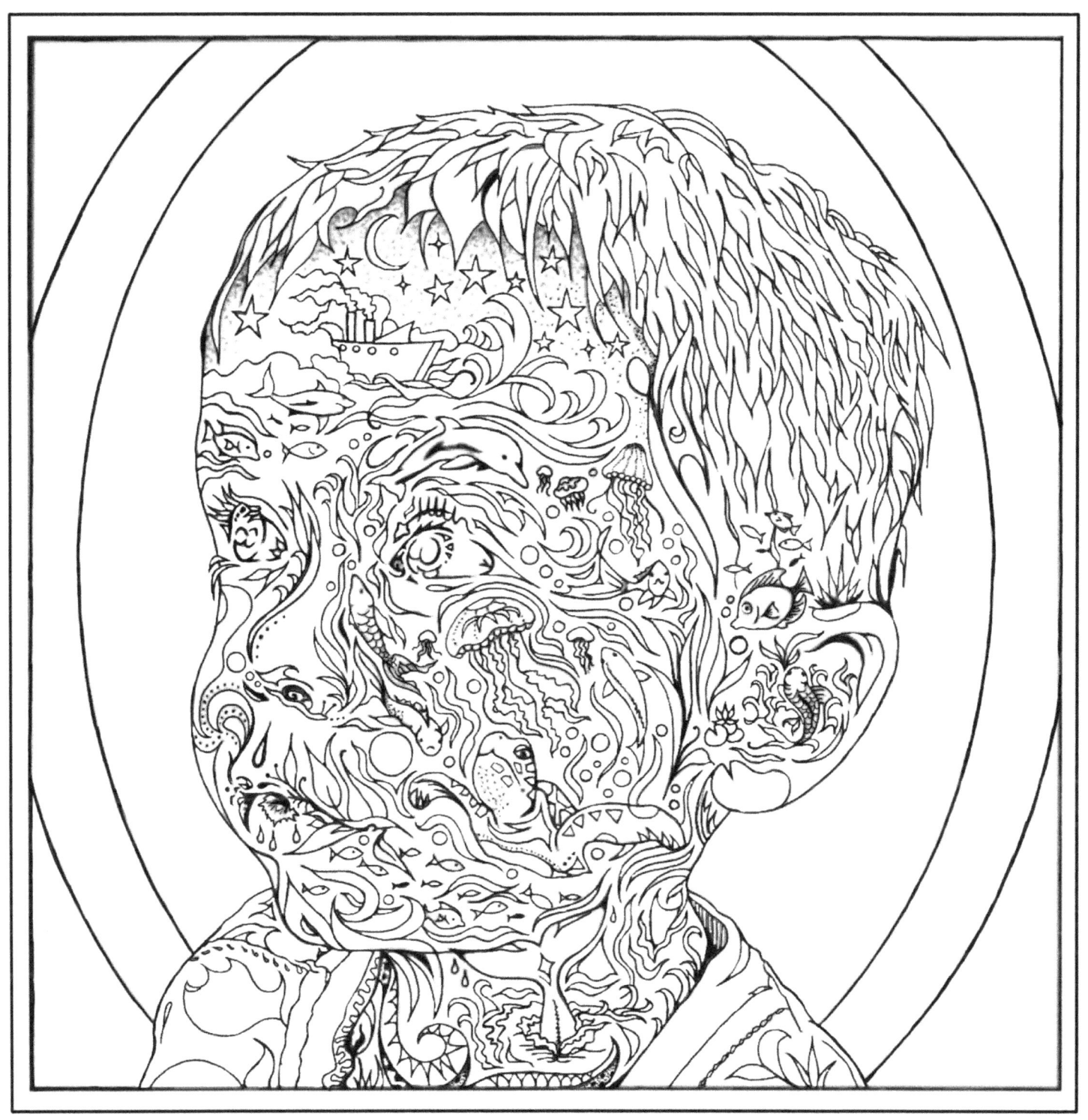

DANIEL

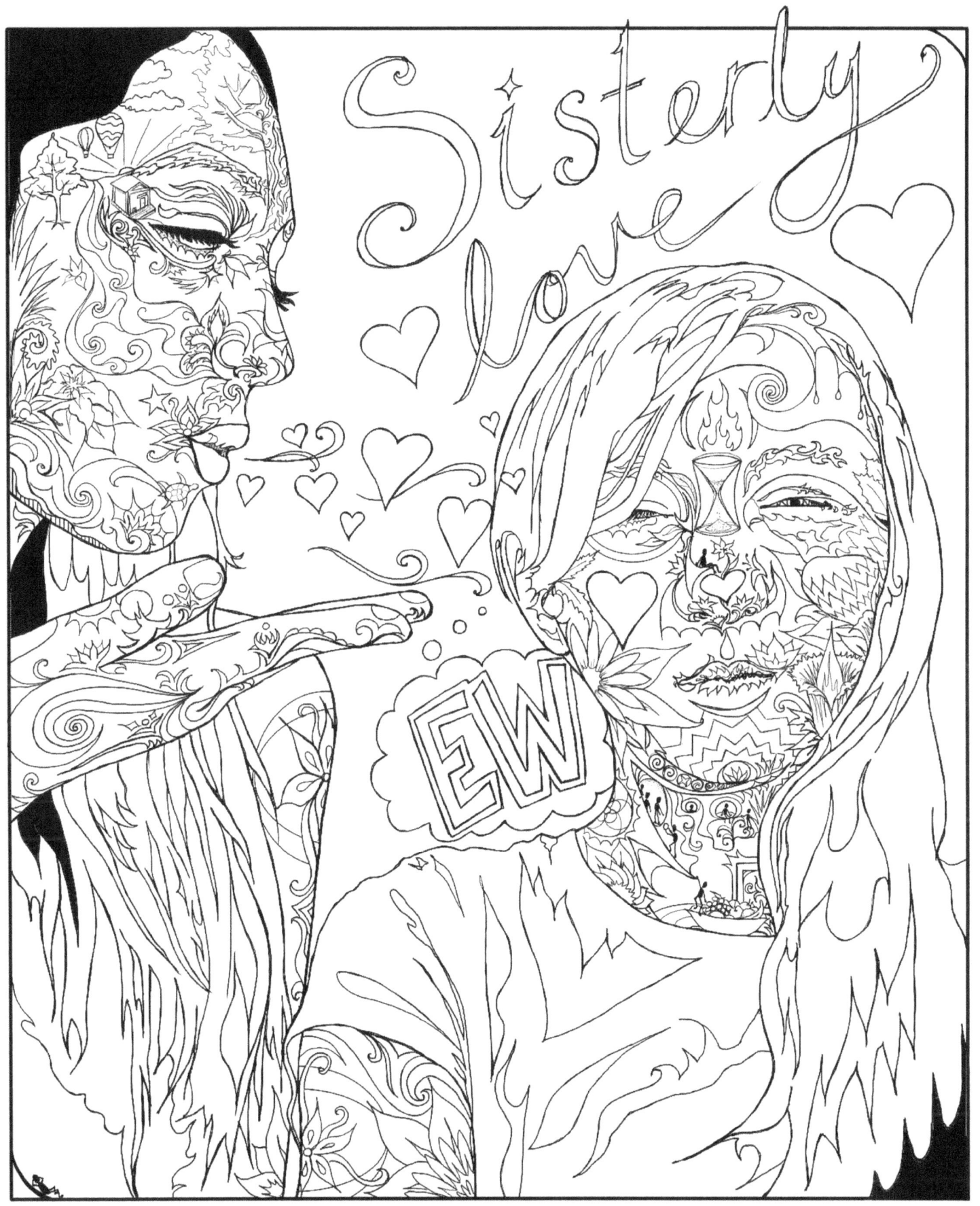

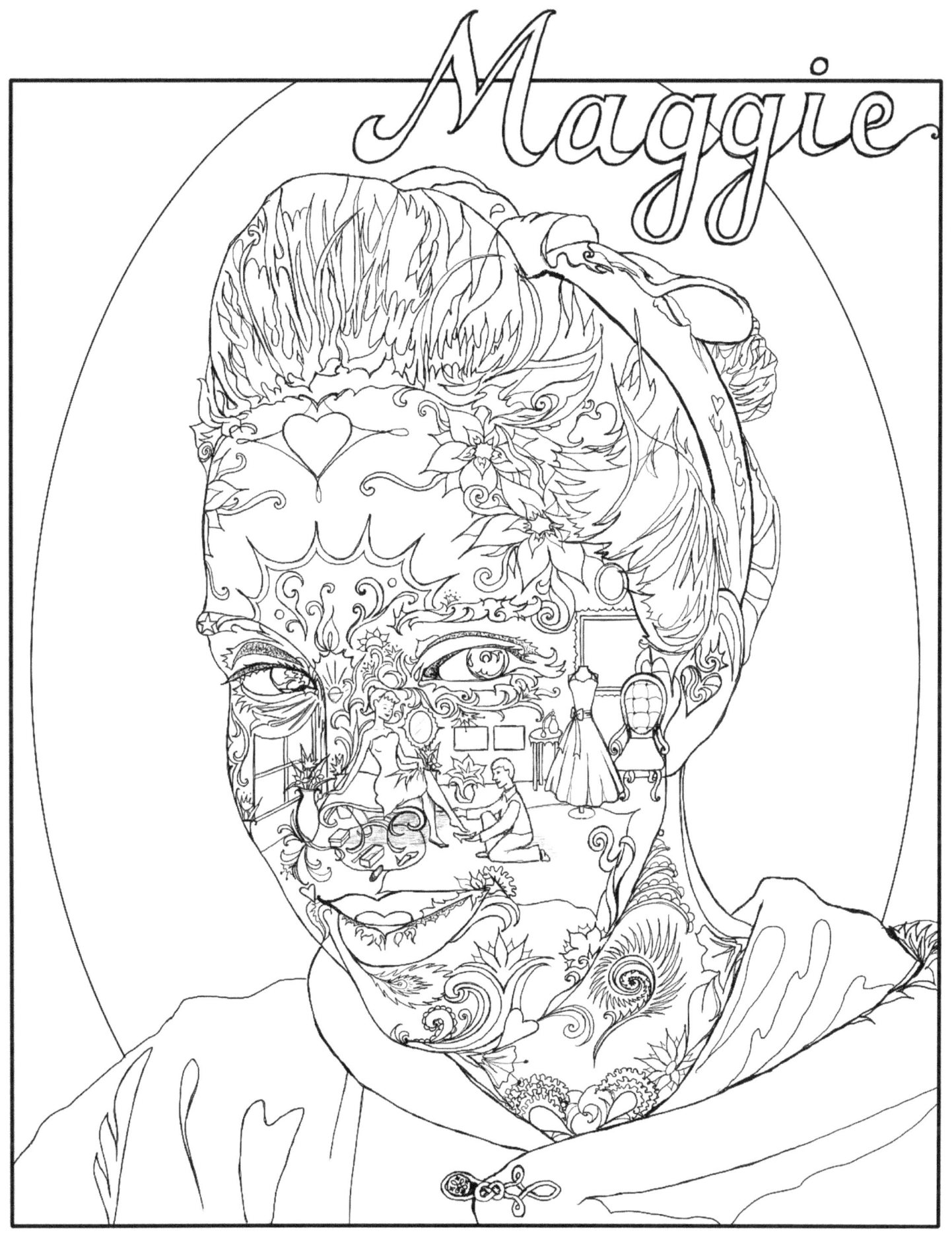

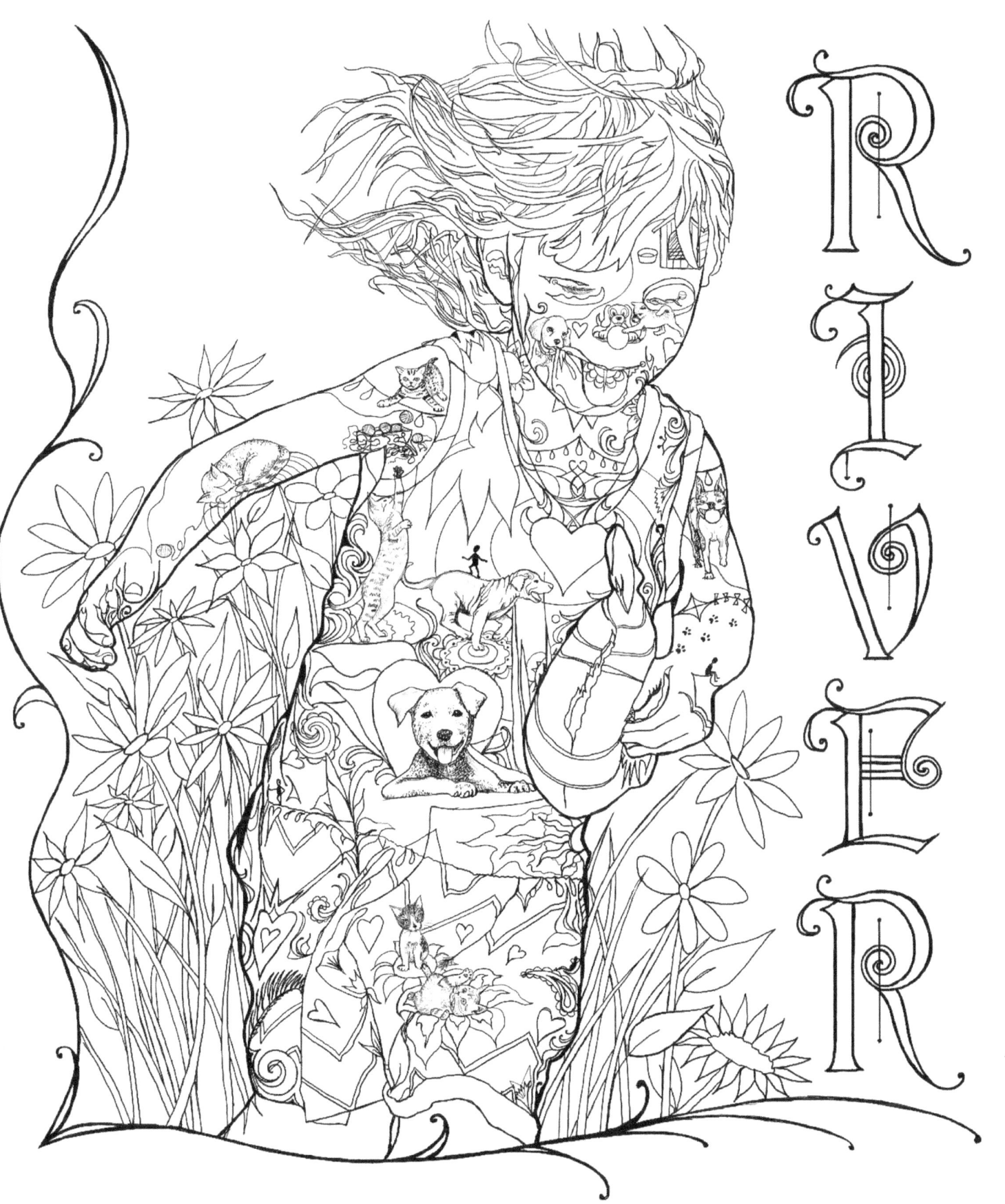

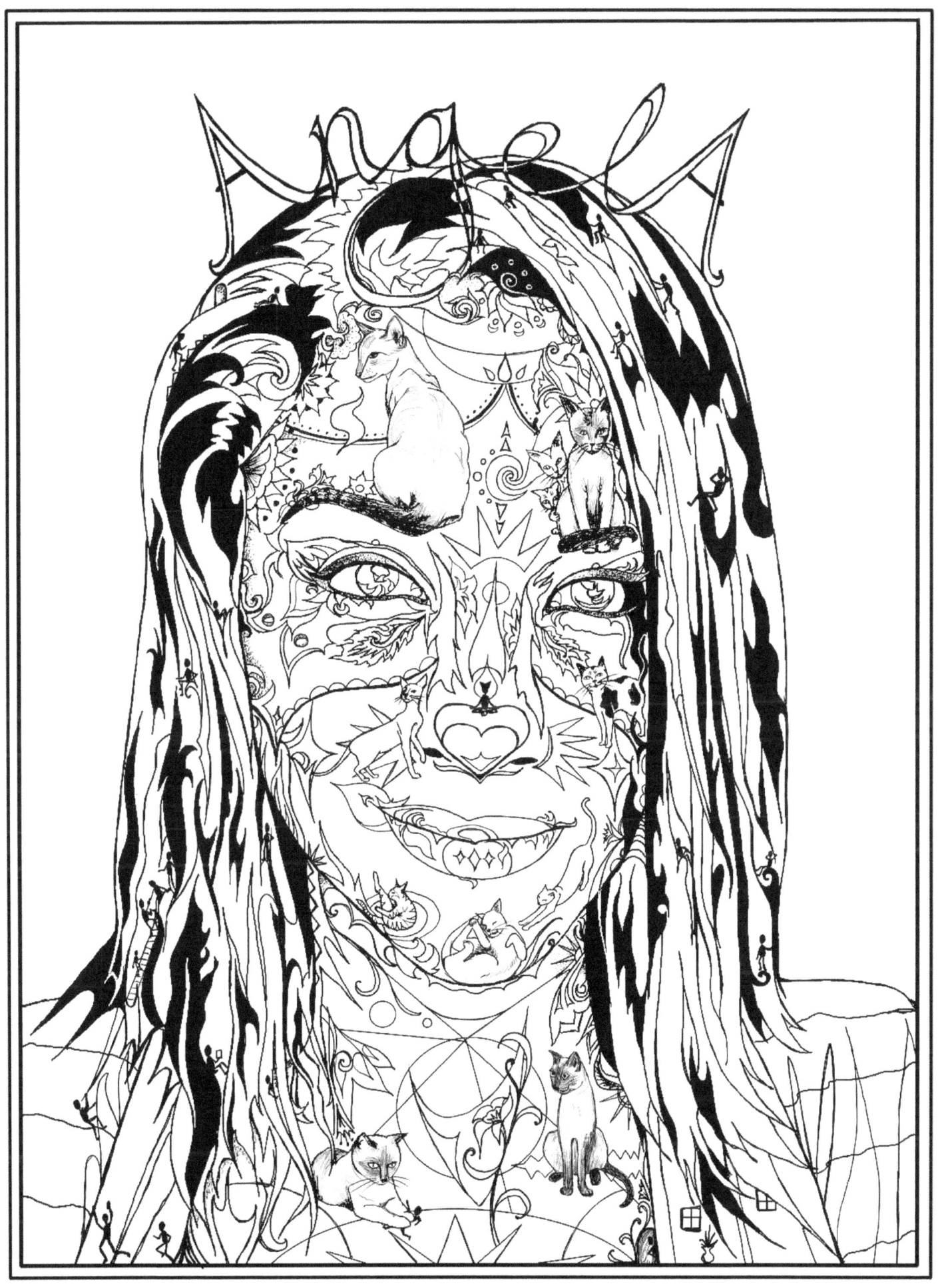

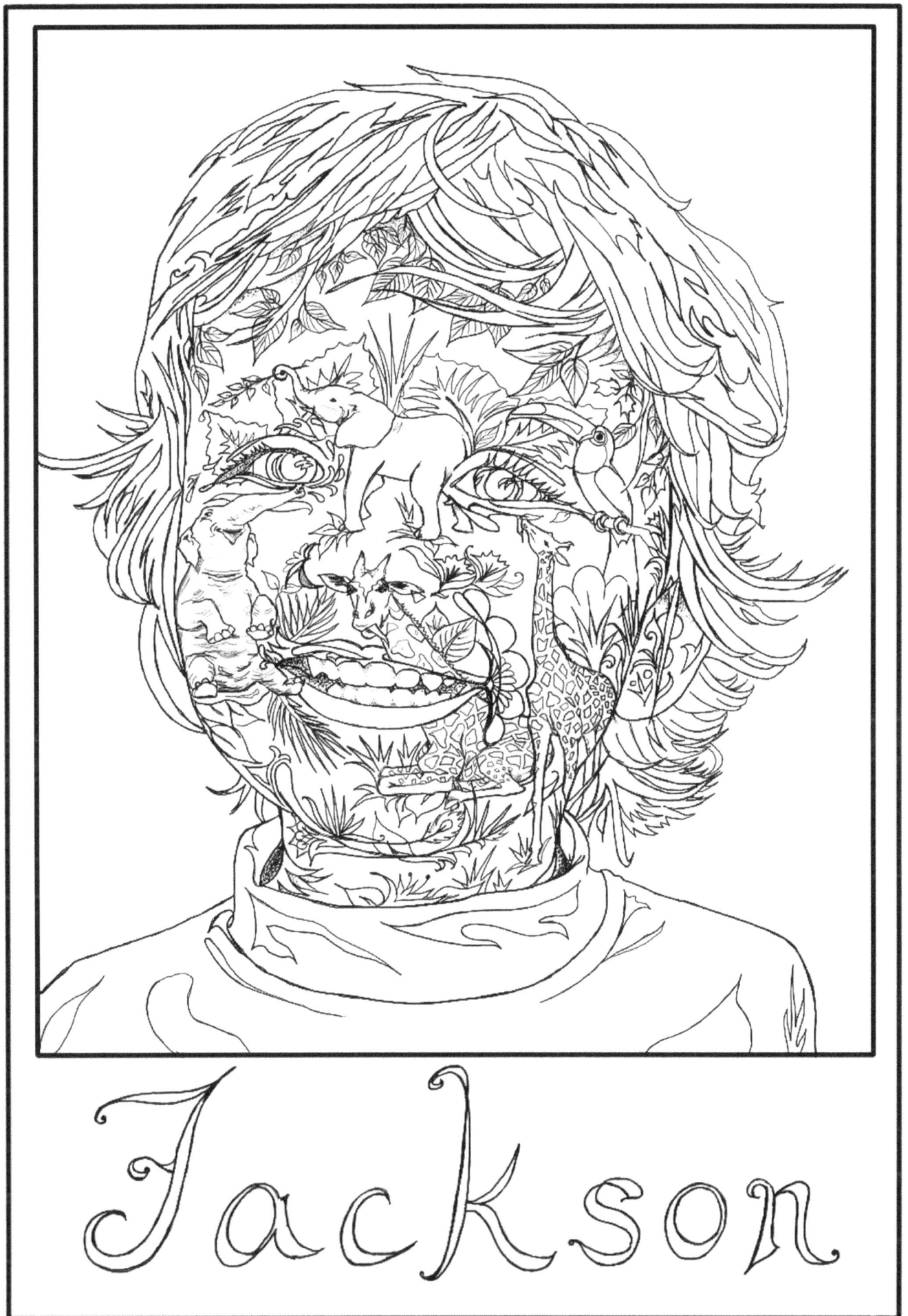

Jackson

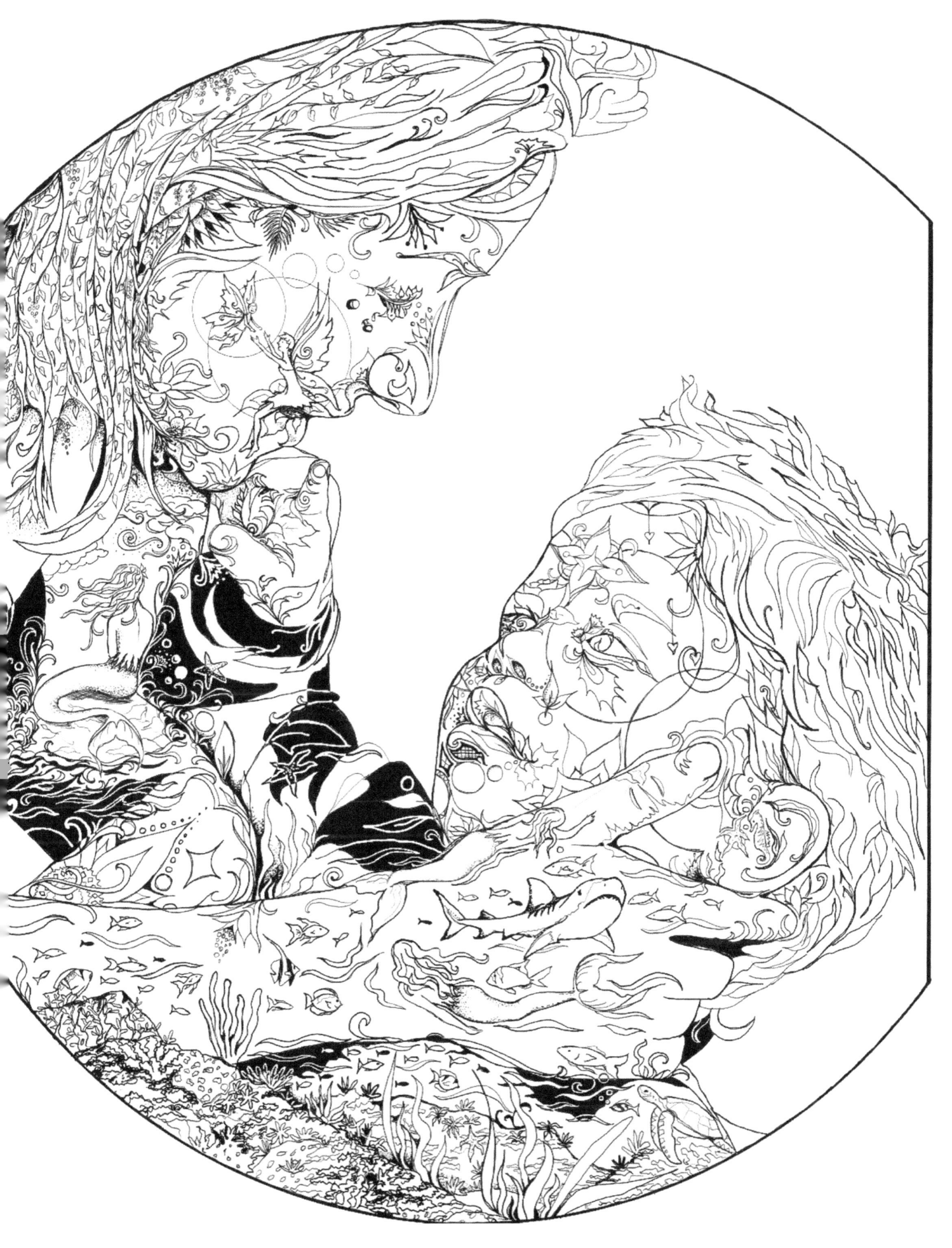

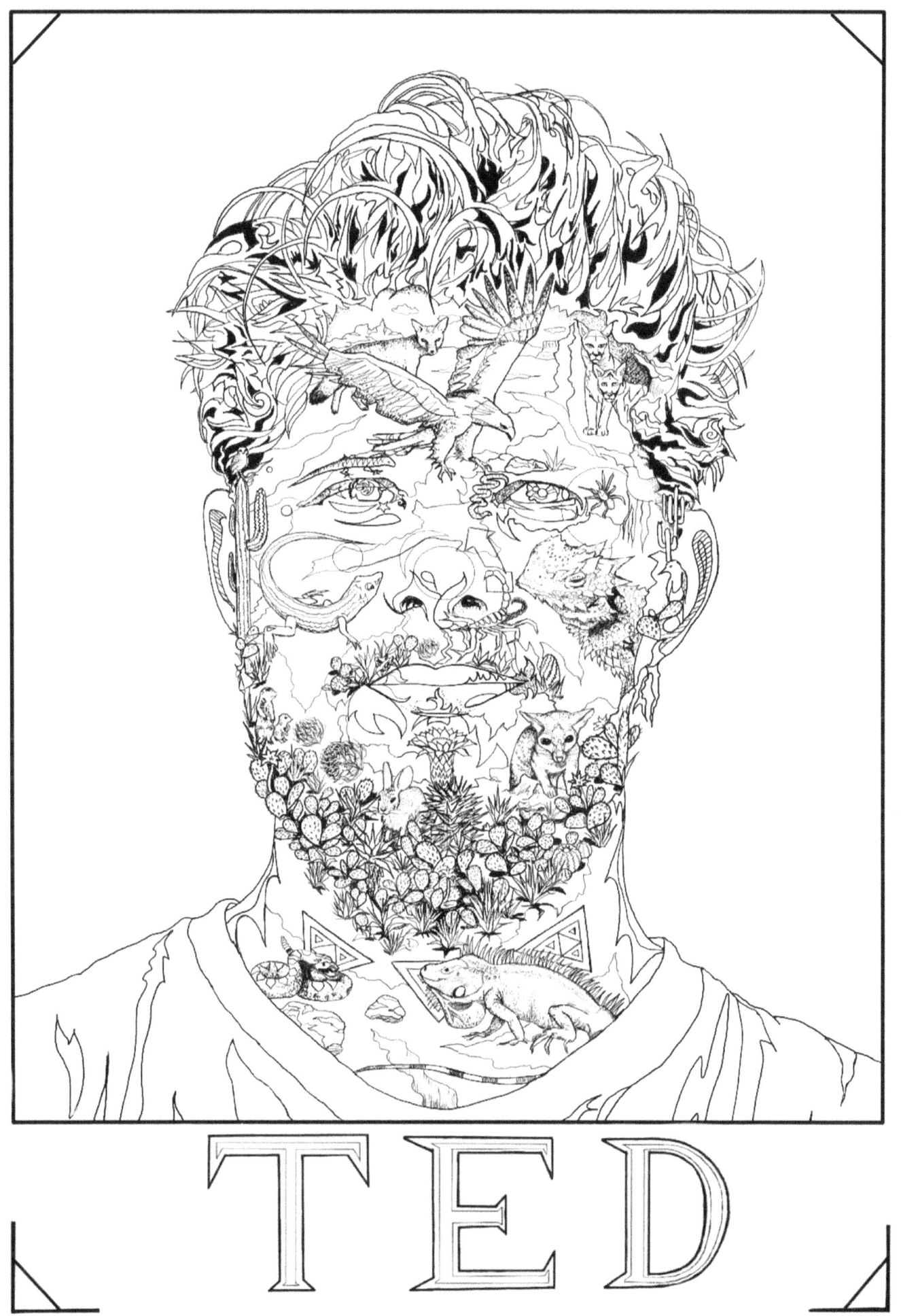

TED

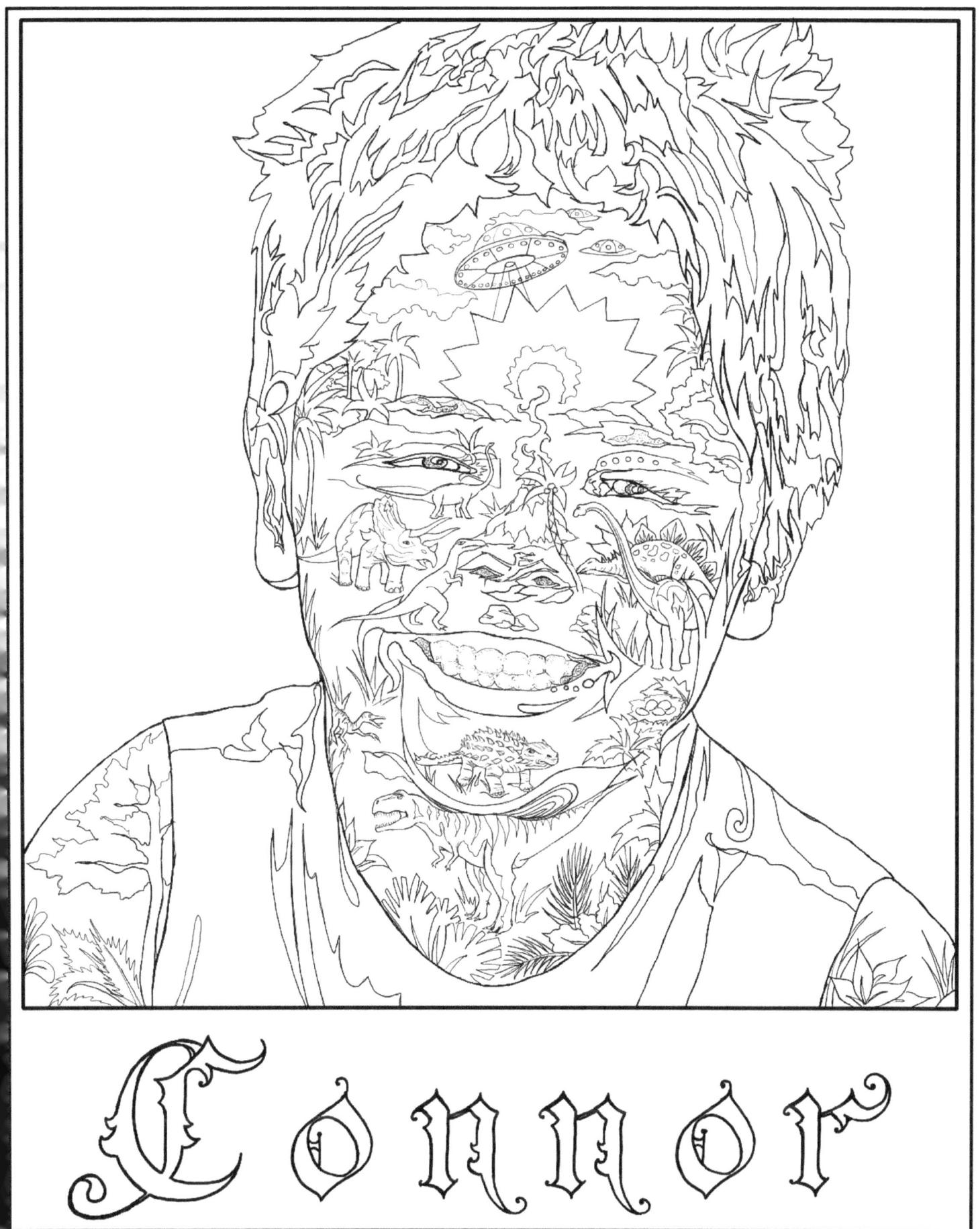

Connor

.

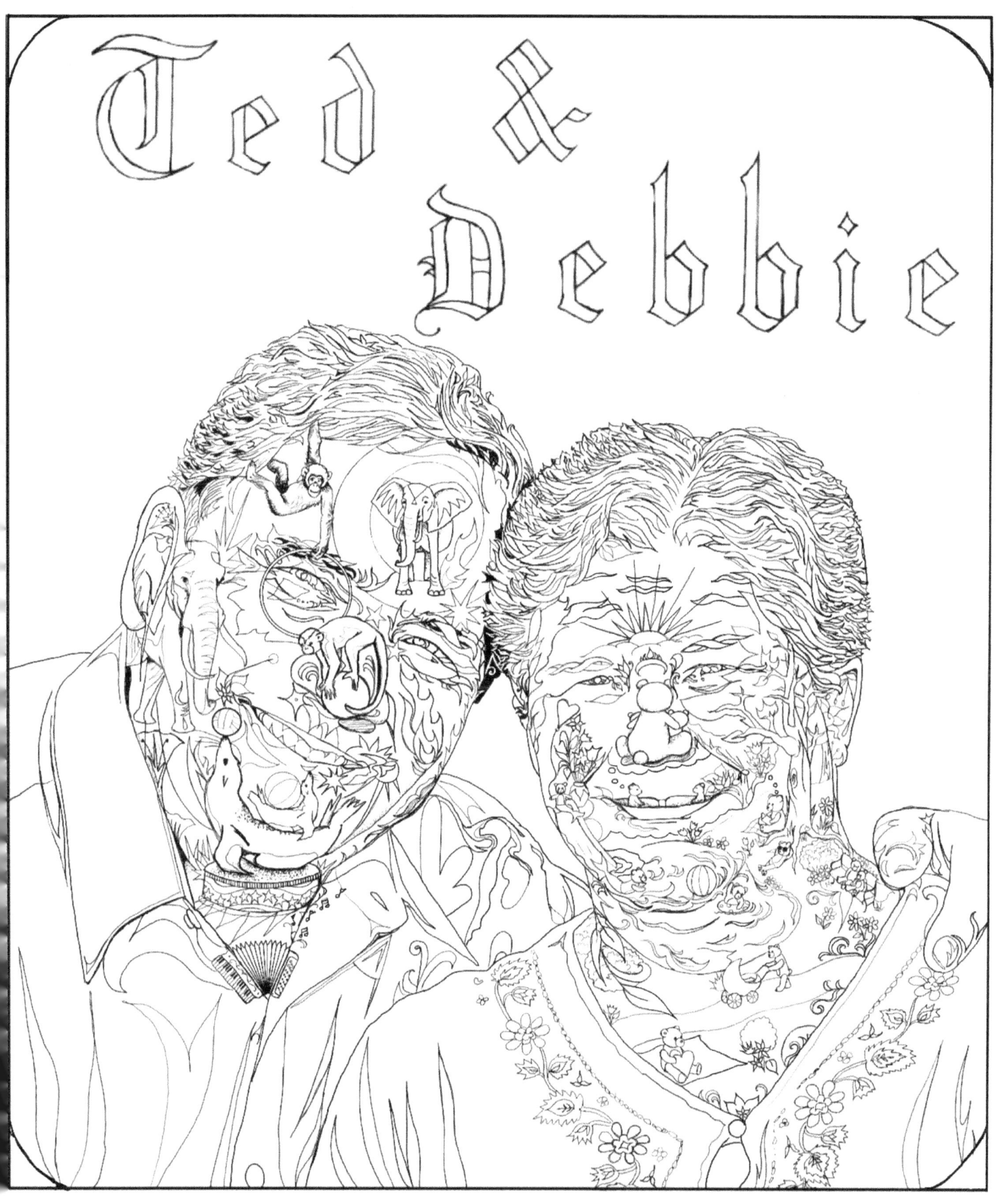

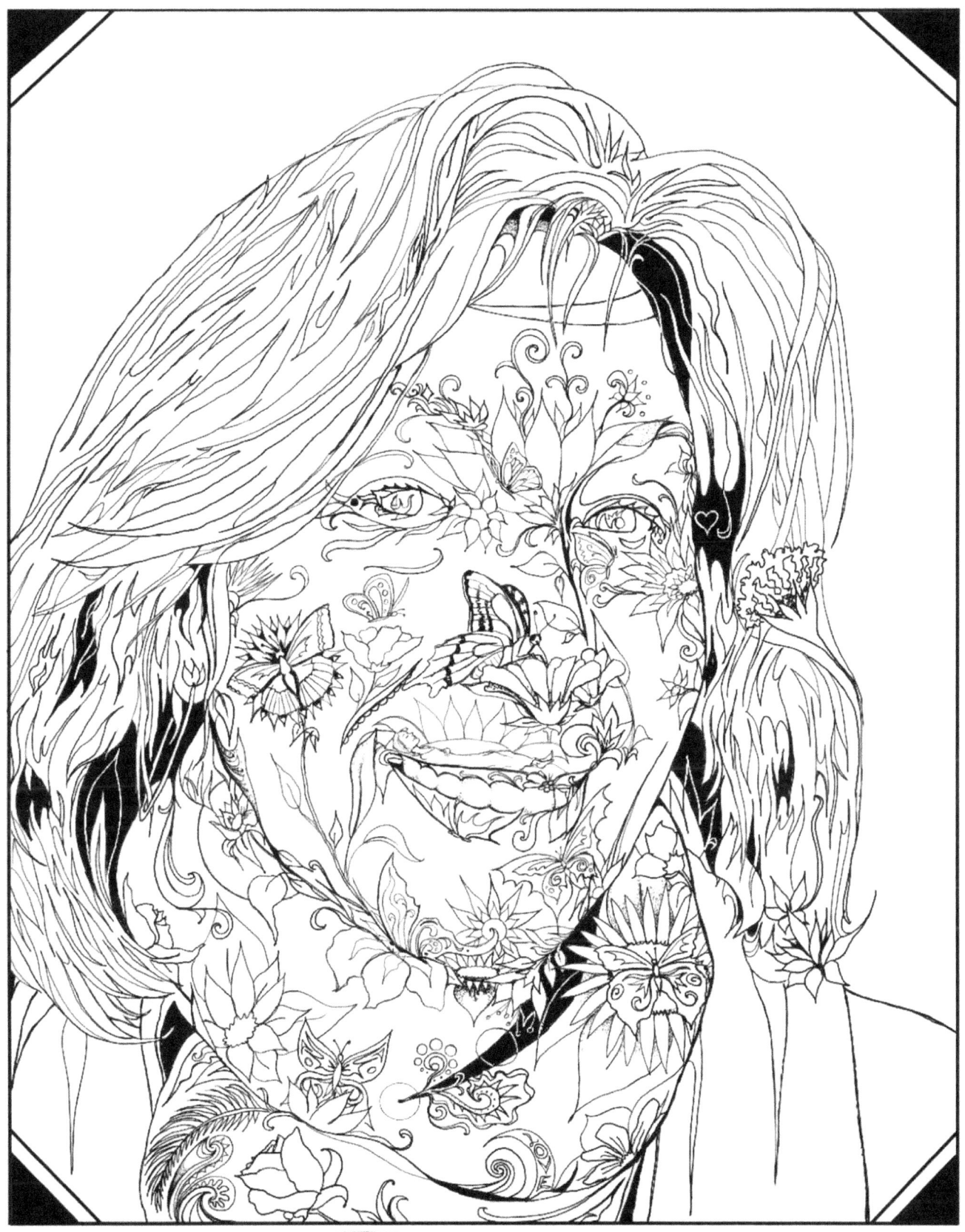

Grace

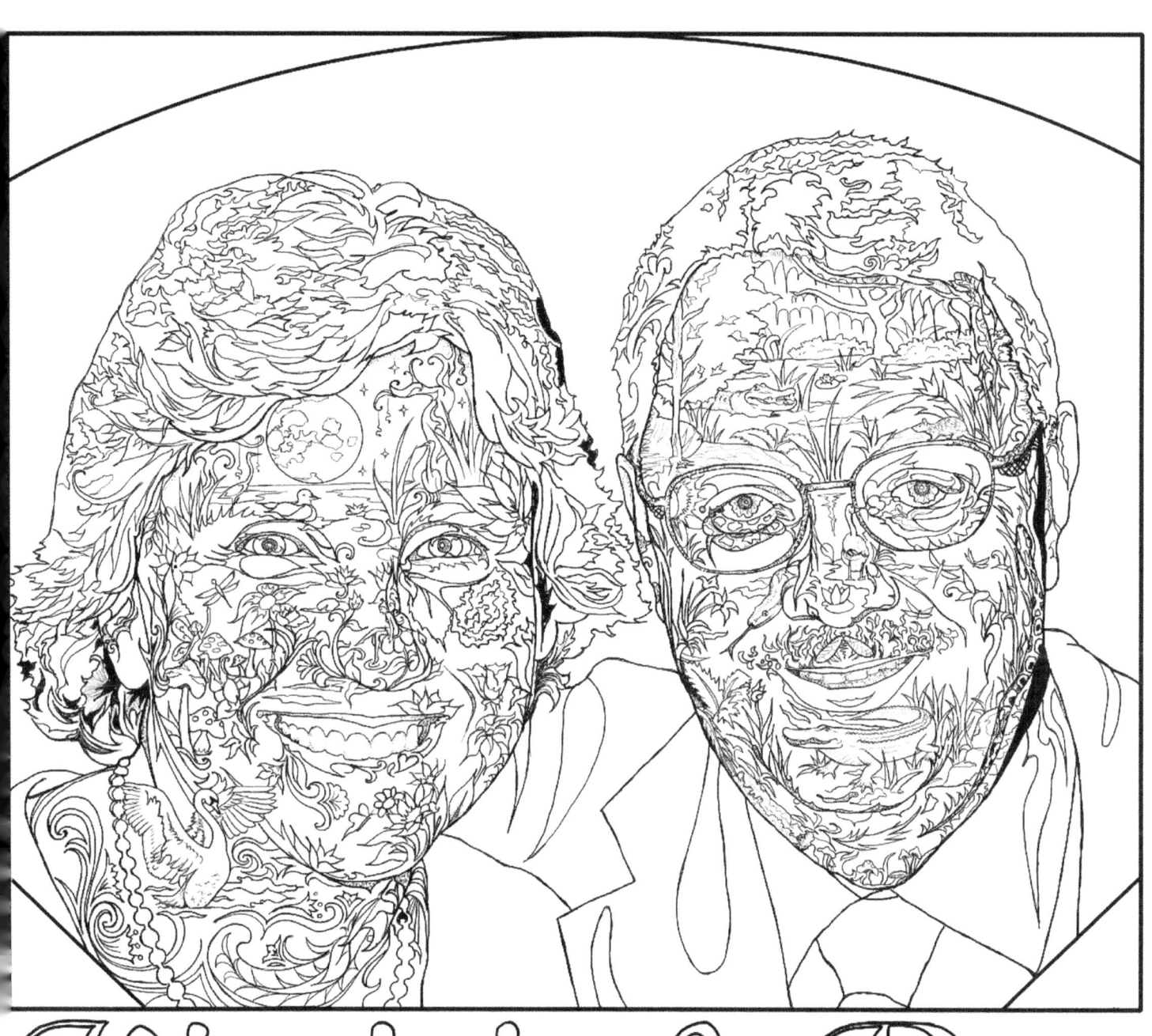

Virginia & Ron

Barbara & Chris

In loving
Memory

Lois &
Richard

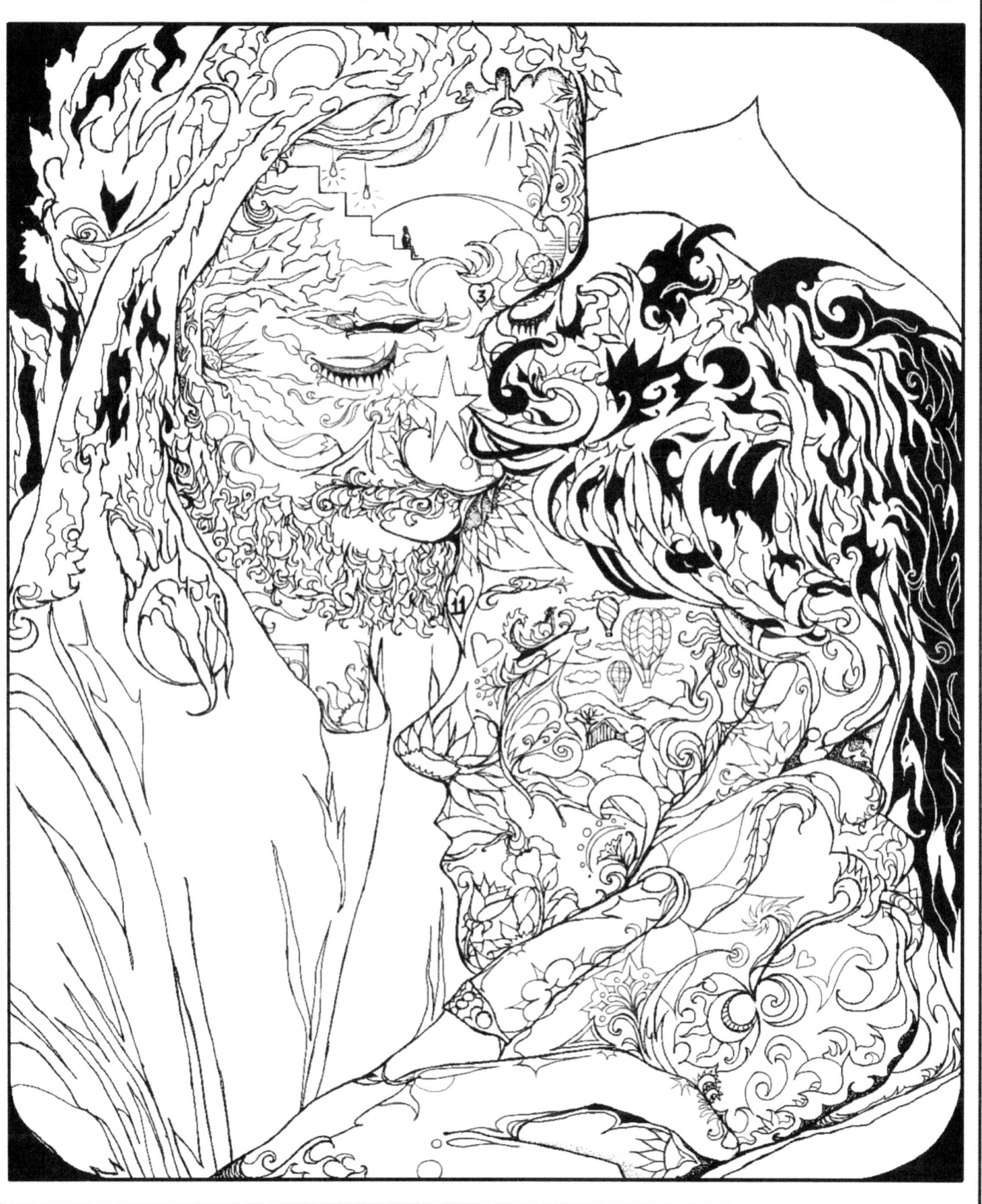

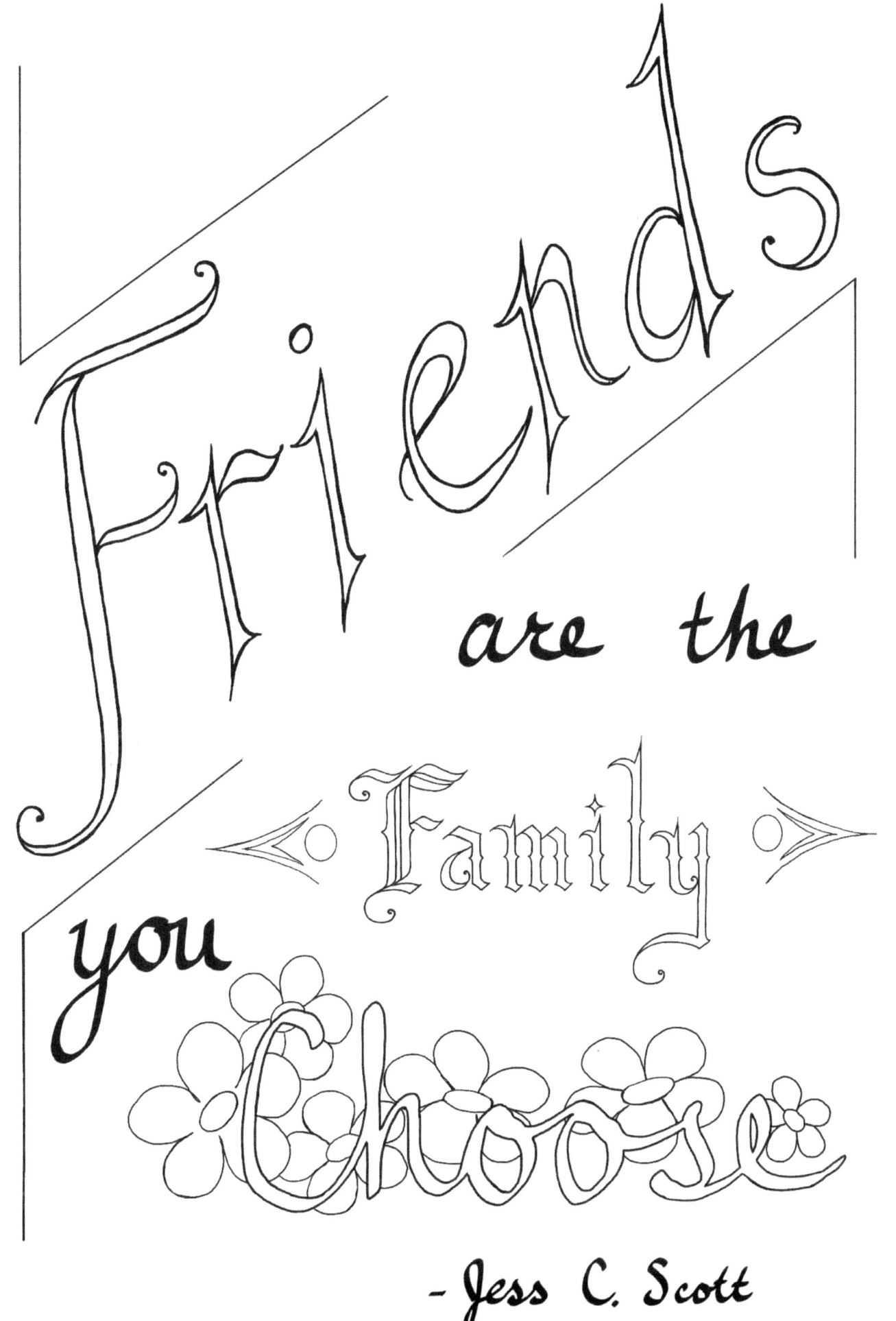

Friends are the Family you Choose

- Jess C. Scott

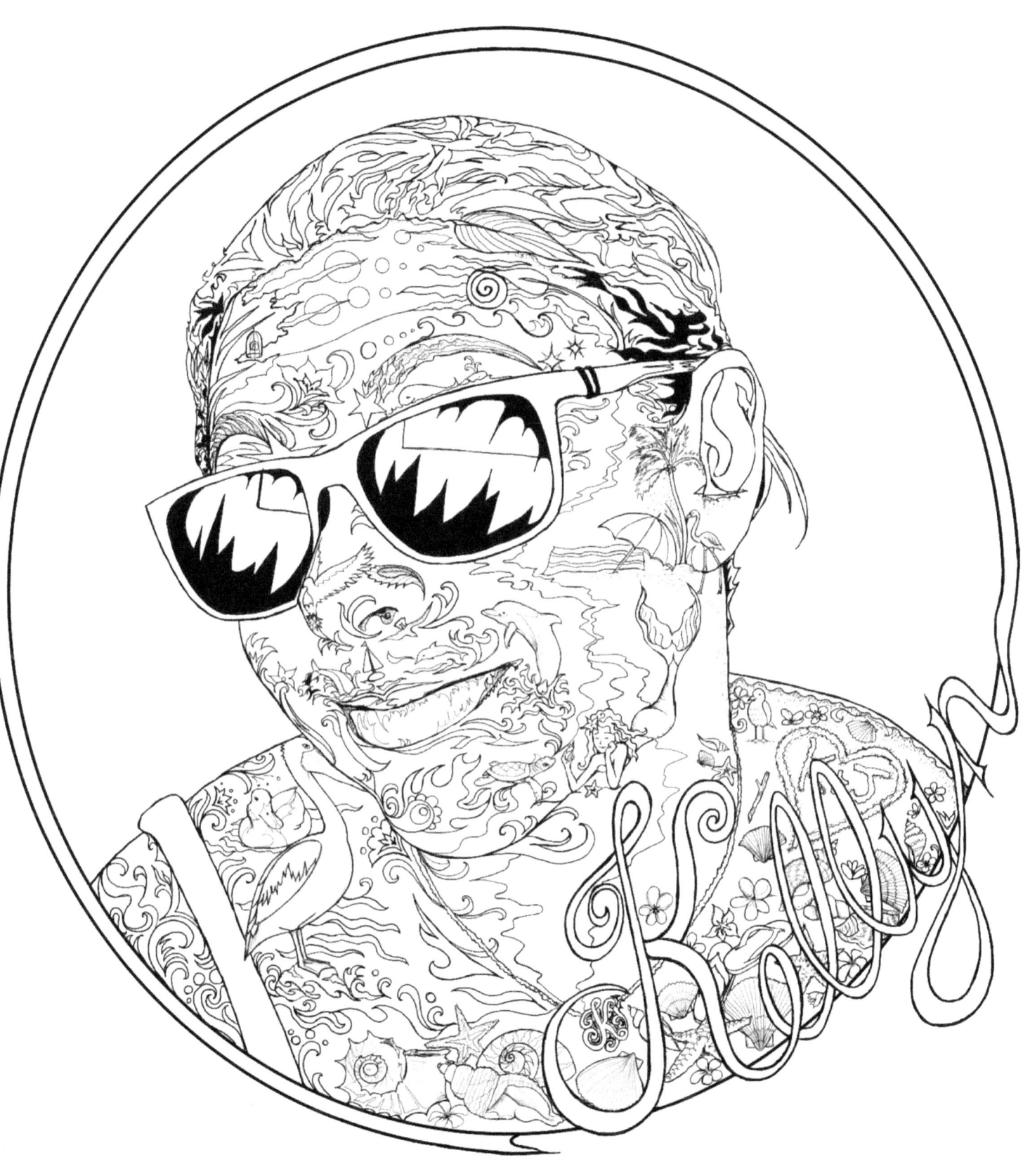

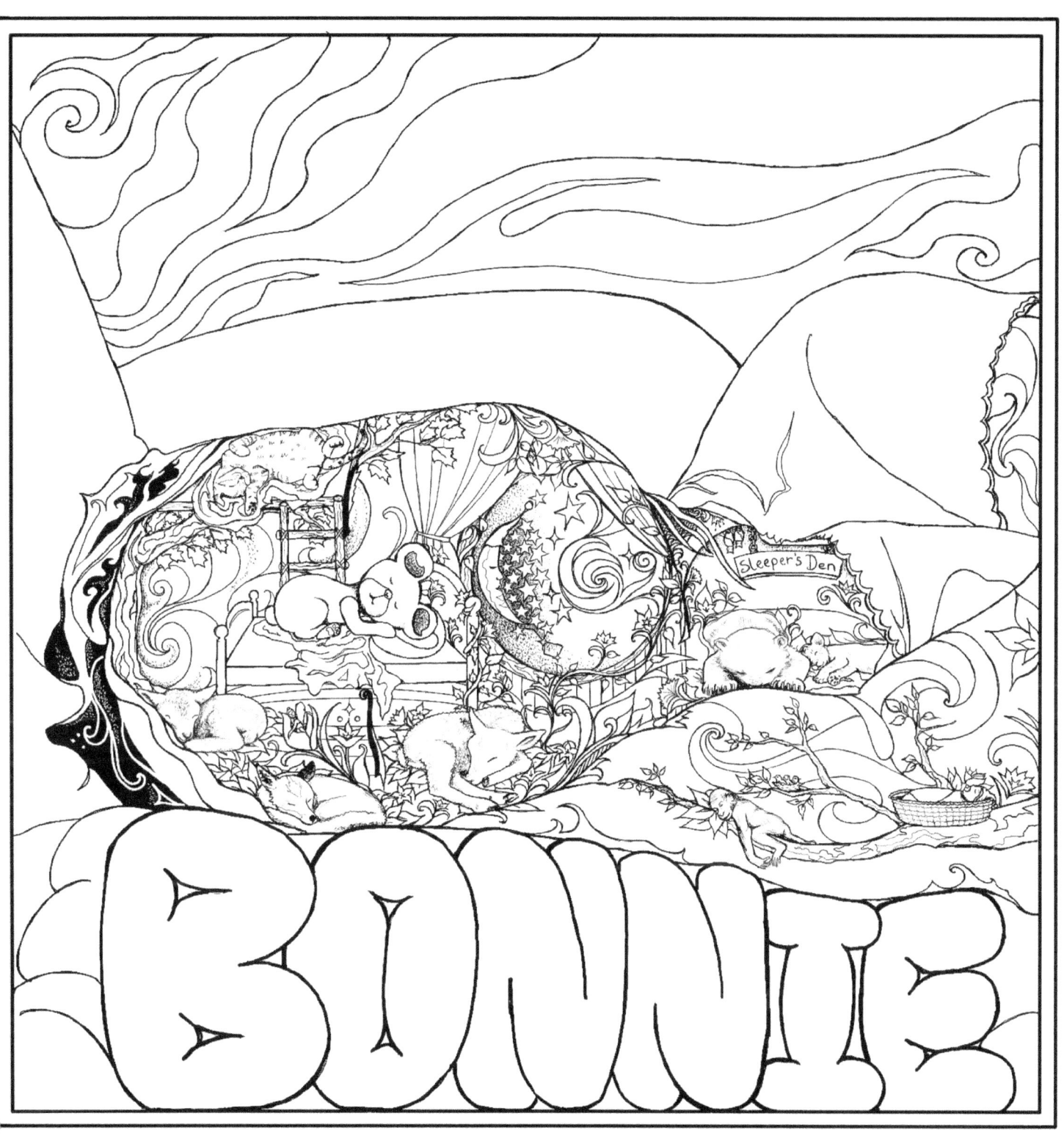

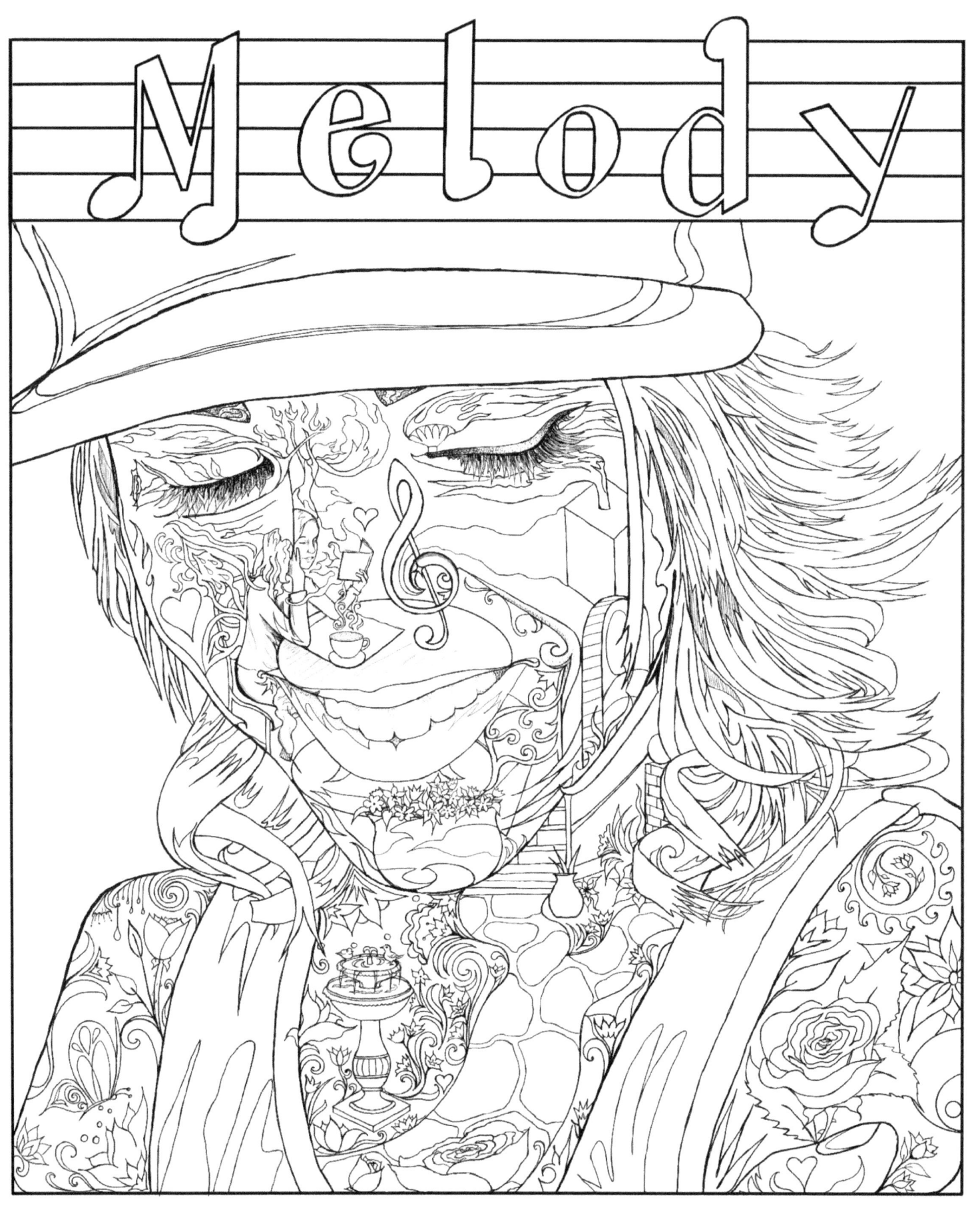

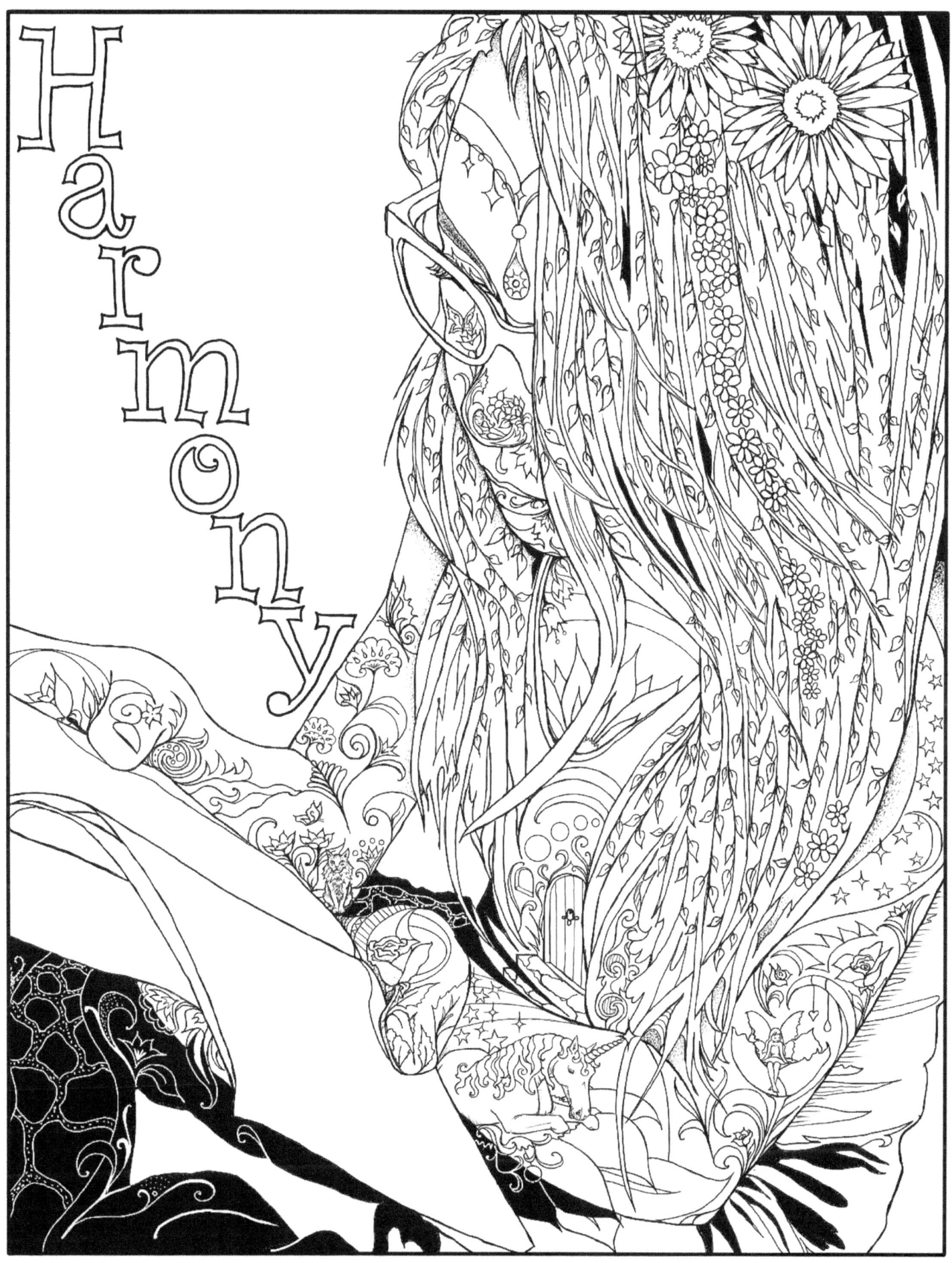

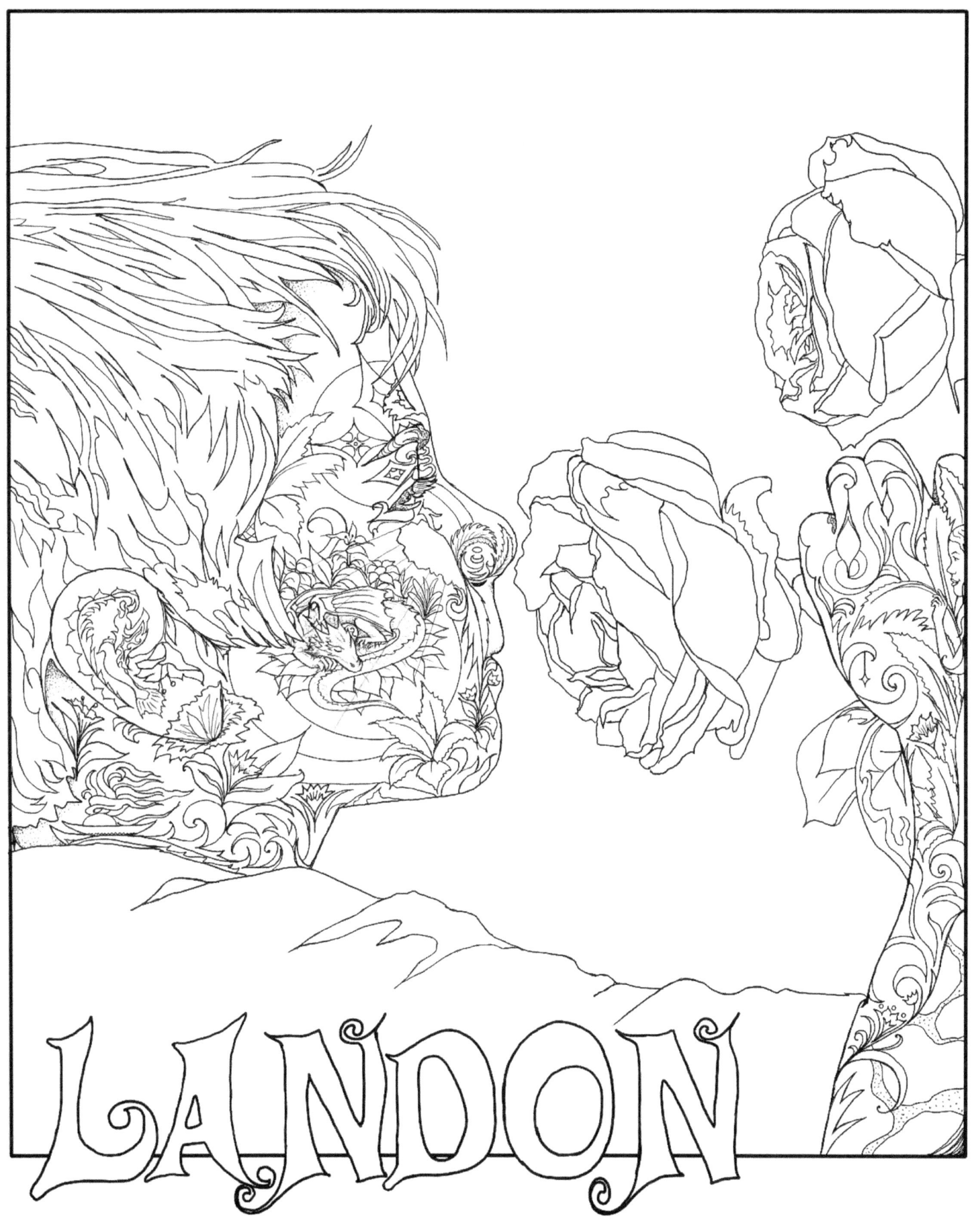

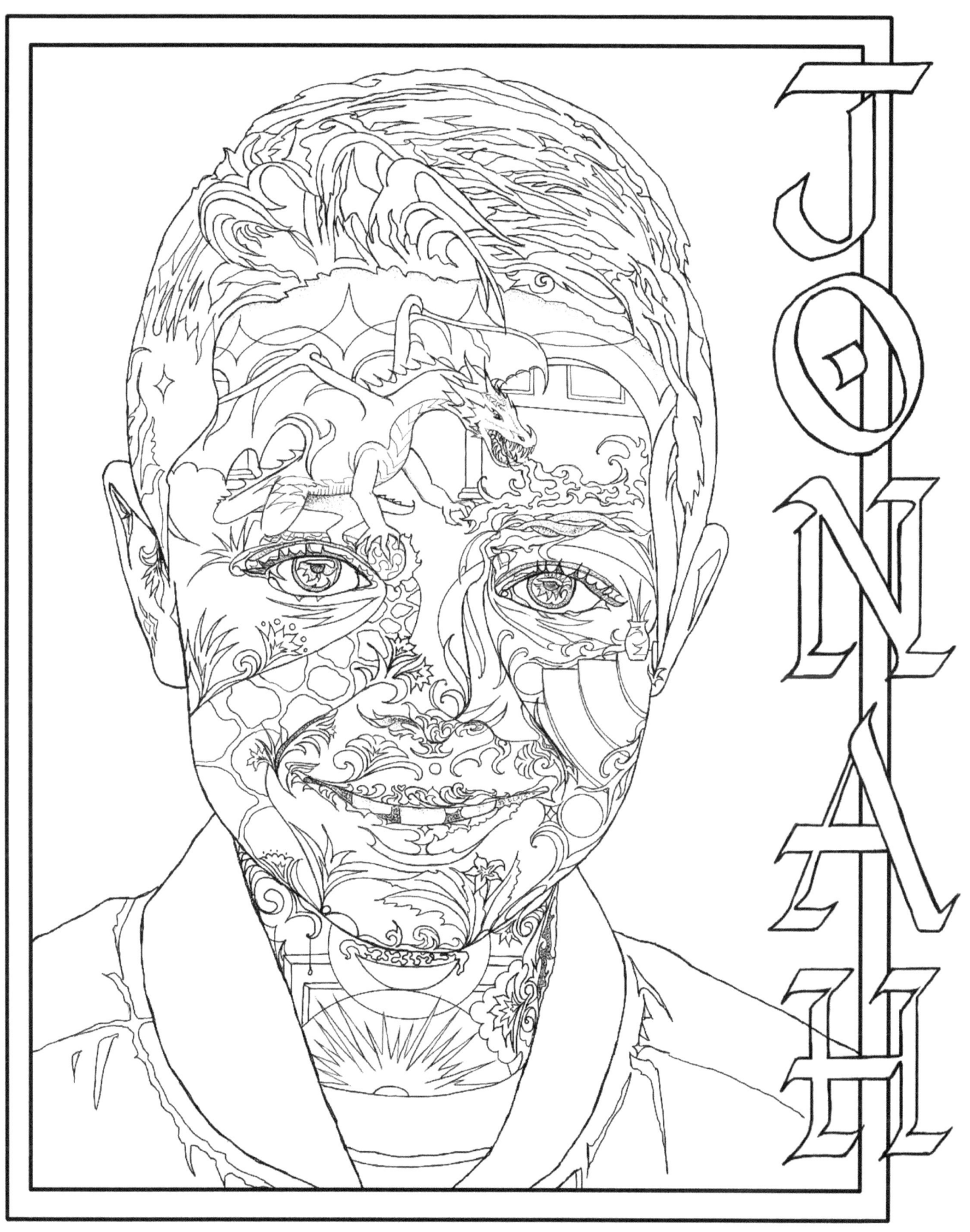

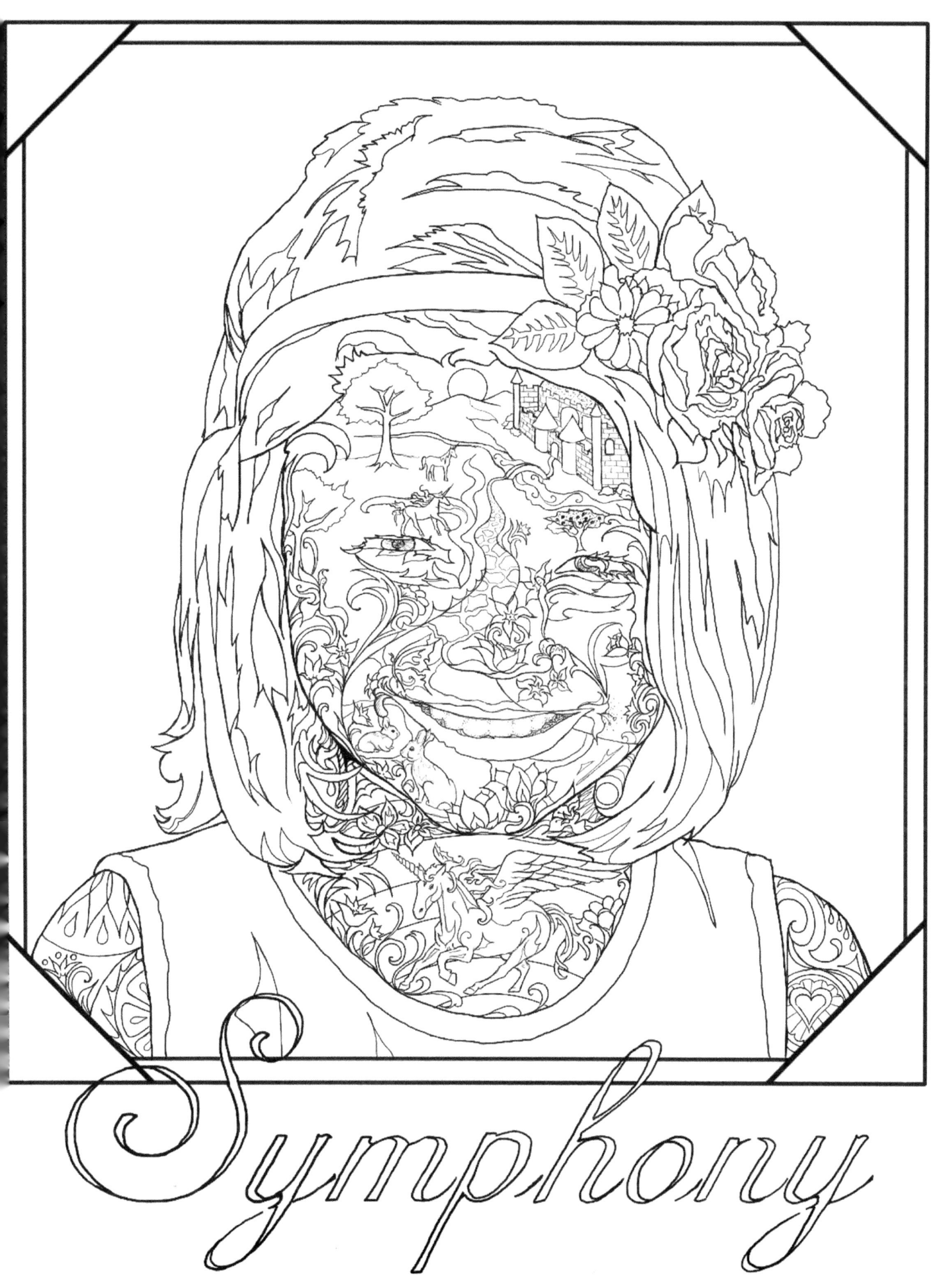

Symphony

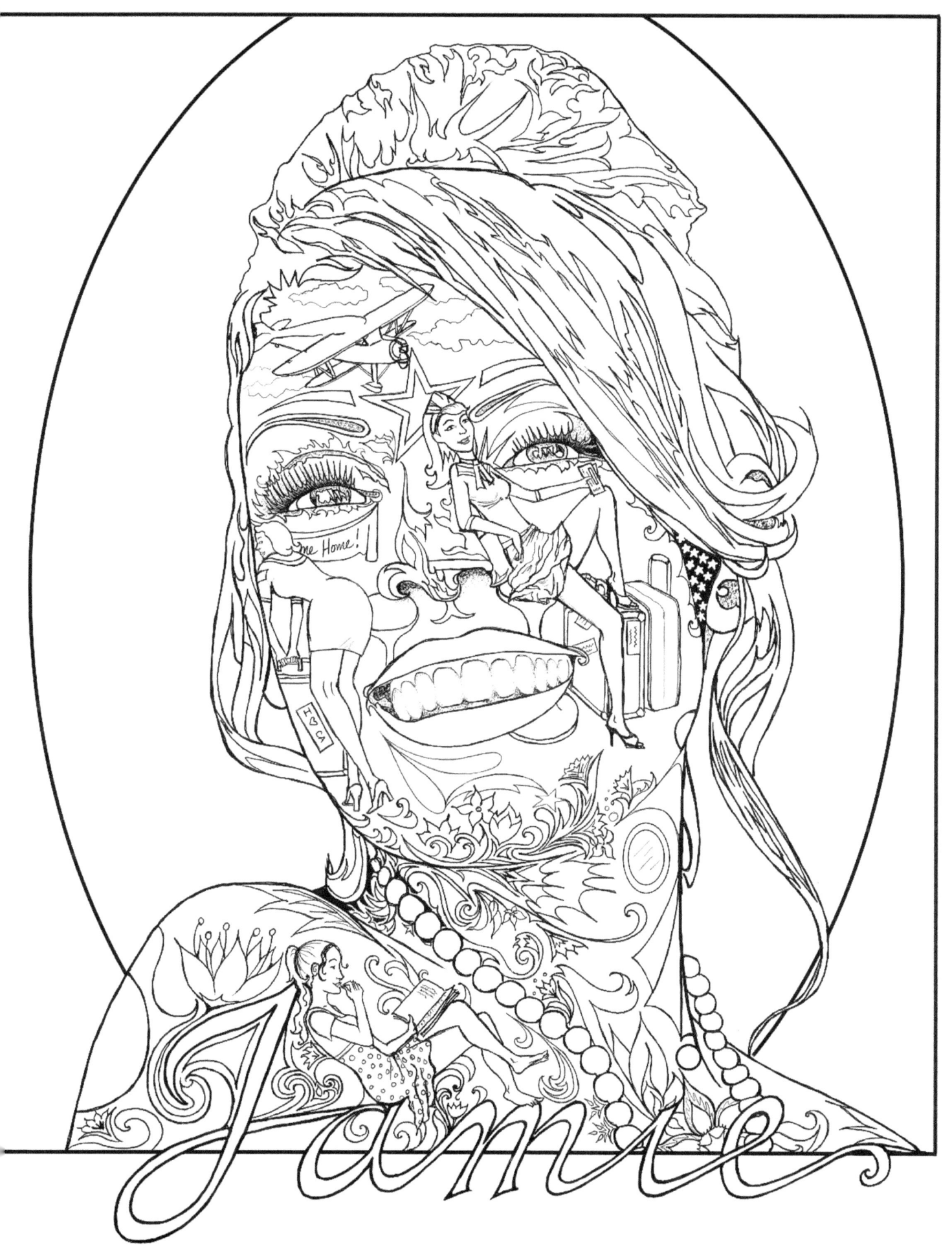

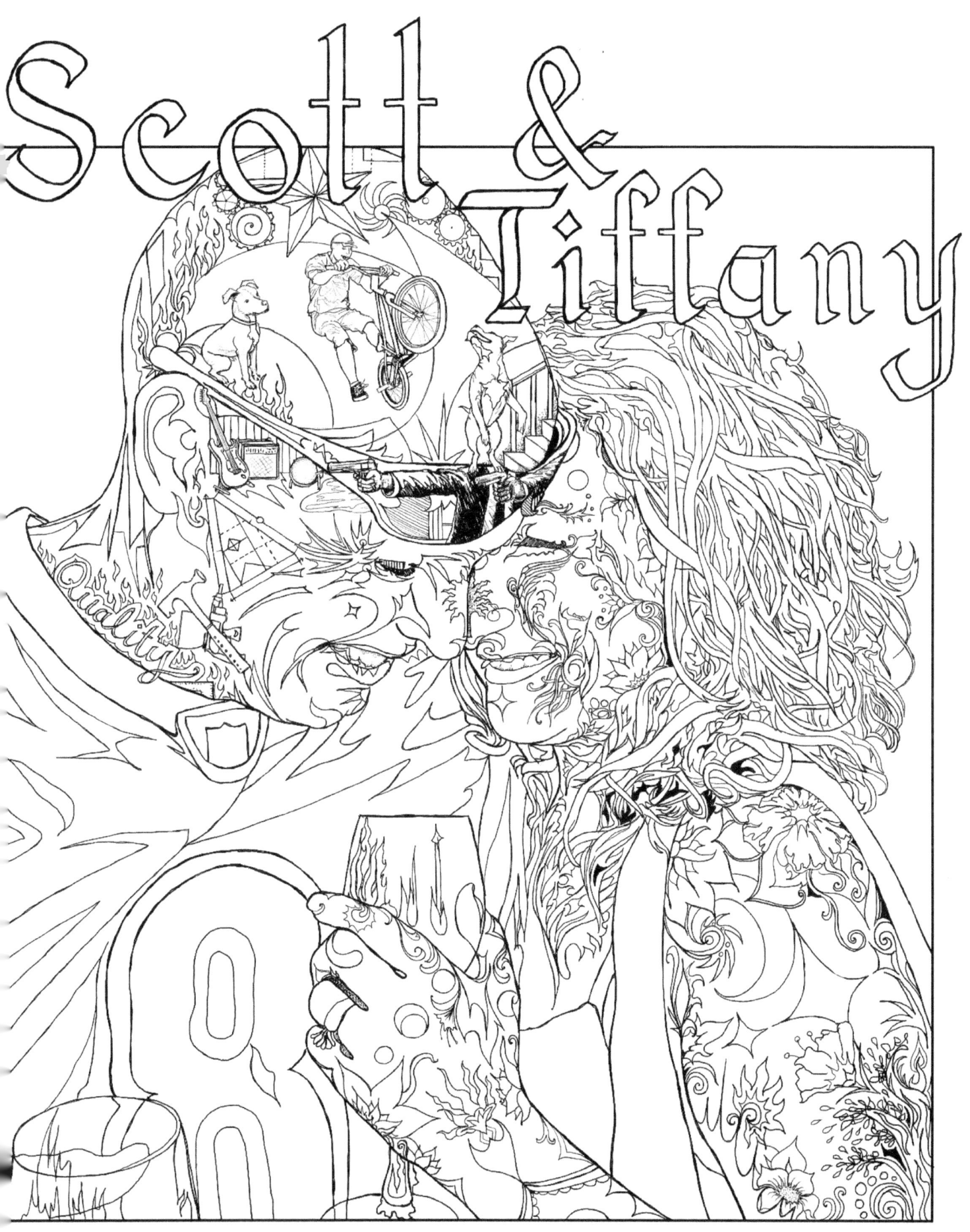

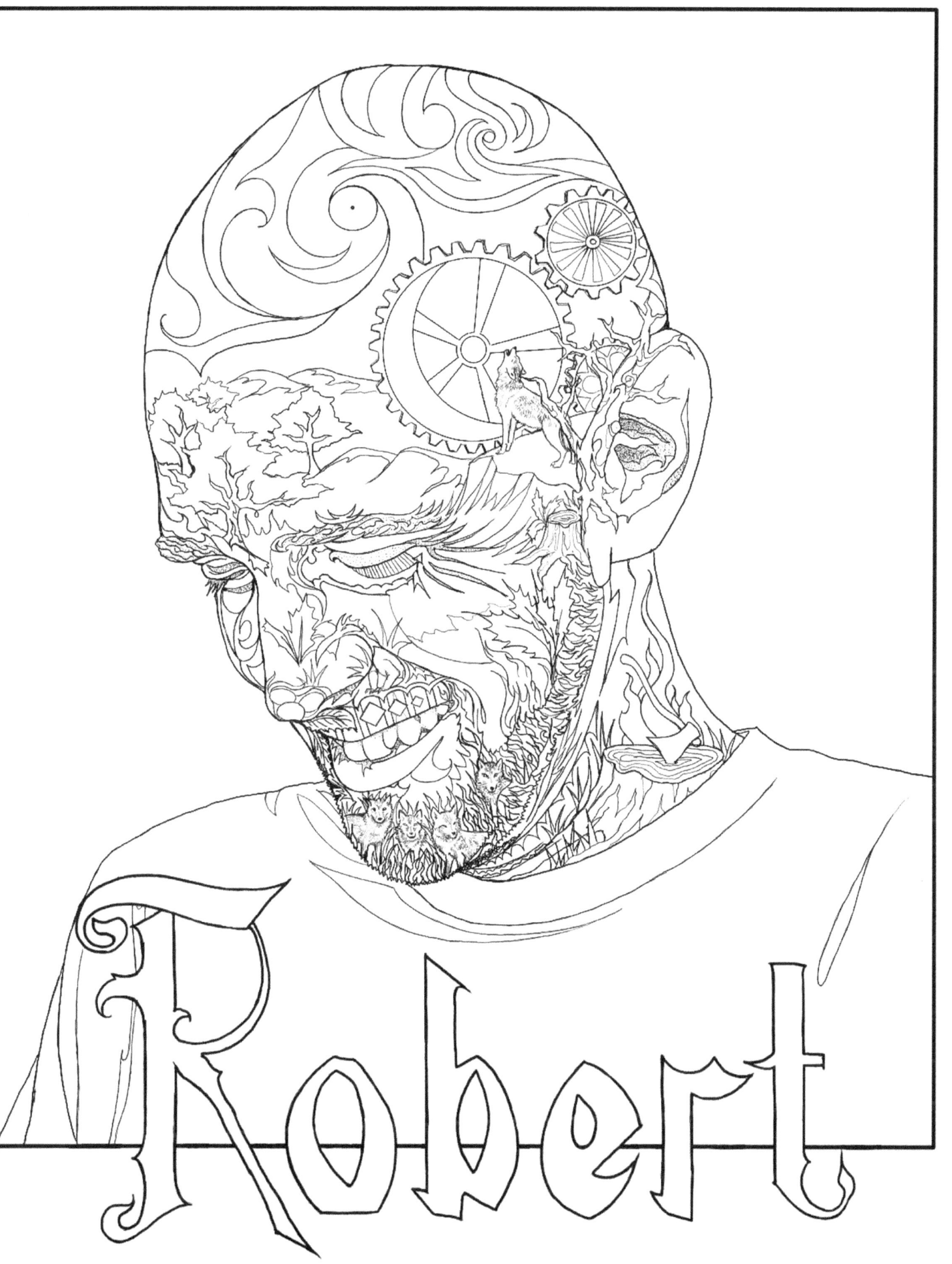

www.ingramcontent.com/pod-product-compliance
Lightning Source LLC
Chambersburg PA
CBHW080544190526
45169CB00007B/2626